How to Manage Conflict

Written by Dr. William Hendricks
Edited by National Press Publications

NATIONAL PRESS PUBLICATIONS

A Division of Rockhurst College Continuing Education Center, Inc.
6901 West 63rd Street • P.O. Box 2949 • Shawnee Mission, Kansas 66201-1349
1-800-258-7246 • 1-913-432-7757

National Seminars endorses non-sexist language. However, in an effort to make this handbook clear, consistent and easy to read, we've used the generic "he" when referring to both males and females throughout. The copy is not intended to be sexist.

How to Manage Conflict
Published by National Press Publications, Inc.
© 1991 National Press Publications, Inc.
A Division of Rockhurst College Continuing Education Center, Inc.

Printed in the United States of America

11   12   13   14   15   16   17   18   19   20

ISBN 1-55852-032-5

Table of Contents

.

INTRODUCTION

Do you carry a map in your car?

A map provides many of us a sense of security, just in case we're ever lost. Maps can sit for years and never get unfolded; others are worn thin at the creases from extensive use. A map can explain unfamiliar territory, but is not something we usually think about until we need it.

Too often this philosophy applies to conflict management. We don't think about reconciling problems or issues until we're lost in the conflict.

This handbook is a conflict manager's map. Each chapter provides directions to get you over rough terrain and through unfamiliar territory. A good map can point the way to possibilities, but it can't solve the problems. That's your job.

Pull up a chair, open this map with me and chart a course of action to manage the conflicts in your life. The ideas presented come from many disciplines. They have been tested by fire during major conflict.

This handbook will help you identify personal attitudes about conflict and map out a perspective for your business. Conflict does not have to create excessive delays in your day-to-day business or cause long career detours; but most important, conflict doesn't have to be feared.

Conflict is frightening for some people. It is a reminder of past failures for others. *How to Manage Conflict* is a practical guide designed to remove the fear that surrounds conflict and give you new confidence by looking at conflict as a commodity that can be managed.

You'll probably find this study of conflict takes you in new directions. I hope you find something that eases the conflict in your life and makes it possible to work more effectively with the people around you.

1

UNDERSTANDING CONFLICT

Conflict, A Fact of Life

Conflict is inevitable! There is a passionate pull inherent in the relationships of life. Humankind always struggles with conflict. Wars have been waged throughout the centuries with little lasting effect, and in the business world, one can scarcely imagine a day without conflict and the stress it causes.

This ever-present conflict demands attention. We need a way to diffuse our fear of conflict. Our business, family and social contacts can be enhanced when conflict is understood. In this chapter, we will define conflict and identify prevailing myths that have restricted our efforts to manage it.

Naming the Territory

Map makers of days gone by labeled unknown territory as the place where dragons existed. For businesses today, conflict is that unknown territory. However, businesses and individuals can't afford to have an unknown territory like conflict. Psychological security is gained when we name the territory of our fears. Therefore, our first step toward effectiveness in managing conflict is to name the territory – become familiar with the unknown.

The Chinese symbol for conflict is a product of two Chinese words: danger and opportunity. Conflict is neither positive nor negative. Resolution can move in either direction. This symbol provides a label for conflict, removing it from the world of the unknown. Conflict does not necessarily mean impending disaster, but includes an opportunity. The territory is manageable!

Myths About Conflict

Myths arise when we lack understanding. They cause us to operate under misconceptions and biased perspectives. It's possible that some myths have invaded your thoughts about conflict. Below are five common myths about conflict.

Five Myths That Inhibit Positive Conflict Management:

1. The presence of conflict is a sign of a poor manager.

2. Conflict is a sign of low concern for the organization.

3. Anger is negative and destructive.

4. Conflict, if left alone, will take care of itself.

5. Conflict must be resolved.

Myth #1: The presence of conflict is the sign of a poor manager. This myth plays on both low self-esteem and insecurity, and pulls a manager into a fear cycle of worry and scurry. The fact is, conflict happens! An effective manager anticipates conflict when possible, deals with conflict when it arises, and enjoys its absence when possible. Relationships are too diverse to effectively judge the quality of a manager on the presence or absence of conflict.

One quality that made Willie Shoemaker an extraordinary jockey was his excellent control. The horse, often unaware of his presence, never felt his hand on the rein unless it was needed. A good manager has this "soft set of hands" during conflict.

Tension will naturally arise as your business relationships are stretched to their limit. Your ability as a manager rises when you respond with the "soft hands" of conflict management, neither judging nor being judged by the presence of conflict.

You will be judged by what you do with the conflict, not by the presence of it!

Myth #2: Conflict is a sign of low concern for the organization. This implies that people expend enormous amounts of time and energy on things that matter little. Generally, people defend and protect those areas where deep concern exists, so conflict indicates genuine concern.

Conflict can help clarify your emotions, and serves as a tool for identifying your underlying values.

Myth #3: Anger is negative and destructive. This myth ignores anger as an emotion, neither positive nor negative, like the wide array of human emotions experienced daily. The energy needed to move in a positive direction comes from the emotions generated by those who care enough to get invovled. Anger is only one letter away from danger, but it also can lead to satisfaction when dealt with appropriately.

Myth #4: Conflict, if left alone, will take care of itself. This is a half-truth. You can avoid conflict – it is a valid coping strategy, but not the *only* strategy. The intensity of conflict varies. Left un-checked, conflict can escalate as easily as dissipate.

Myth #5: Conflict must be resolved. This myth stifles creativity, causing the manager to become solution-oriented. Some conflict is best managed by endurance, while other events require multiple solutions. Quick movement toward resolution can limit success.

This excessive focus on a solution can be counter-productive. Single-focused thinking that sometimes happens when we believe we must find a solution can cause a loss of perspective. Failure to see the big picture while coping with a particular problem, even a major one, can become a major pitfall during conflict.

Summary

Competent business people often become ineffective during conflict, held captive by the power of such myths. The goal is to explore the territory known as conflict, name it, and weaken the control of exaggerated emotions (myths) that surround it. We are now ready to take the next step in conflict management: assessment.

2

IDENTIFYING CONFLICT STAGES

The Big Picture

Picture a fire house. Shiny trucks, folded hoses, coats, boots and hard hats line the walls. There's a brass pole in the center of the room and a Dalmatian. Each piece is polished and ready for use. A fire department is prepared and ready to respond.

Too many business people are caught looking for the fire hoses during conflict. Effective conflict management results when you are able to develop and implement a deliberate conflict strategy.

The chart on the next page illustrates three distinct stages of conflict. It should help you picture conflict as a series of events that can be managed. If the conflict is identified early and deliberate steps are taken to modify events and manage the emotions, almost any conflict can become a source of opportunity. Left unchecked, conflict is dangerous to you, your people and your business.

Three Stages of Conflict

Stage One

Stage Two

Stage Three

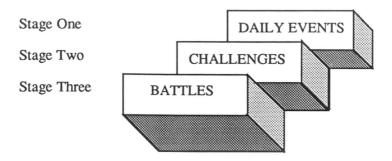

Stage One conflict is the least threatening and easiest to manage. As conflict escalates to stages two and three, it becomes more difficult to manage and the potential for harm increases.

Conflict moves between stages, but it does not necessarily follow a linear pattern. A Stage One conflict on Monday morning, left unattended, can escalate to Stage Three by the end of the day. Conversely, high levels of conflict may dissipate with time, quite unexpectedly. Given this fickle nature, the following list of a conflict's underlying characteristics can provide you with additional insight.

Characteristics of Conflict

1. As conflict escalates, concern for self increases.

2. The desire to win increases with a rise in self-interest. Saving face takes on increased importance at higher levels of conflict.

3. Nice people can become harmful to others as conflict increases.

4. Conflict management strategies that work at low levels of conflict are often ineffective, and at times are counterproductive at higher levels of conflict.

5. Conflict may skip levels.

6. People are likely to be at different individual levels during conflict, but an overall organizational level of conflict can be identified.

Looking for Solutions

A one-alarm fire does not require full gear and every truck in the house. The intensity of a fire determines the response of a fire department. Conflict and the intensity it presents determines the strategy you should use.

The three stages of conflict require different management strategies.

- A Stage One conflict and the accompanying emotions can best be addressed with coping strategies.

- Stage Two requires more training and specific management skills.

- At Stage Three, intervention is necessary.

Characteristics of Stage One

Stage One conflict is ongoing and generally requires little action. Most individuals employ coping strategies unconsciously, and these coping skills are an excellent tool at this level. But coping strategies, like tolerating the actions of co-workers, are most effective when they are deliberate rather than unconscious.

This stage is characterized by day-to-day irritations. These irritations can be passed off, sometimes indefinitely. But an irritation can become a problem. A conflict management strategy at this level should notice if and when this shift from irritation to problem occurs.

The variable that causes irritation to become a problem is people. Different personalities, coping mechanisms and ever-changing life events make it impossible to predict when an individual has had enough. When the shift occurs an alarm should sound, alerting the individuals to bring out the "conflict squad."

Avoidance is one effective coping strategy for day-to-day irritations. We pass things off rather than deal with them because they're minor. You employ avoidance with your boss when you decide that silence might be a better tactic than discussion. The deliberate coping strategy of avoidance happens when you determine there is neither time nor motivation to alter the idiosyncrasies of another. If your contact with the person is minimal, the chances are good that you have managed the irritation appropriately. At this stage a "live and let live" attitude works pretty well.

Think back to your grade school playground, when teams were picked and friends paired off. Instantly, a coping strategy was initiated by those doing the choosing and those chosen last. The games went on, but feelings of alienation were sometimes generated. Similar feelings are produced during daily contacts with other people. One too many irritations can cause problems that must be solved.

Obliging is a slightly stronger form of avoidance, where an individual "gives in" to another. Obliging involves one's desire to "fit in" and belong. This desire to belong is usually strong, and overrides lower levels of conflict. This strategy uses a give-in attitude so things can keep moving. Deliberate obliging can be beneficial to team effort, but there is no way to predict how long an individual will oblige.

Conflict at Stage One is real, although low in intensity. When people work together, differences exist in goals, values and individual needs. At Stage One, parties feel discomfort and possibly anger, but are quick to "pass off" these emotions. Individuals are usually willing to work toward a solution during Stage One conflict, often with a sense of optimism that things can be worked out.

This optimism might be detected as a "no big deal" attitude. Facts and opinions are shared openly with one another once the problem has surfaced. Communication is usually clear, specific and oriented to the present because the people and the problem are not intertwined as they are in more intense conflict.

This distinction is significant. The easiest way to discern whether you are in a Stage One conflict or a more intense level is to observe participants' ability to separate people from the problem. Brainstorming and creative problem-solving work well at Stage One because participants are willing to discuss problems rather than personalities.

Listening and participation are essential at this level. As a conflict manager, initiate joint listening and exploration ventures with an emphasis on teamwork and shared responsibility. This strategy focuses all the participants in a common direction and allows everyone to contribute.

Ways to Handle Stage One Conflict

1. Initiate a process that examines both sides. Can a framework be built that encourages understanding of one another?

2. Ask if the reaction is proportional to the situation. Is either party carrying residual emotions from another event? (Example: Ask each party to consider if this event is isolated or whether the feelings reflect previous disagreements.)

3. Identify points of agreement and work from these points first, then identify the points of disagreement. Is it possible to leap the hurdle of conflict by seeing the whole picture?

Characteristics of Stage Two

Conflict takes on the element of competition at Stage Two, typified by a "win-lose" attitude. Losses seem greater at this stage because people are tied to the problems. Self-interest and "how one looks" become very important. A "cover your hind-end" attitude can also be observed. At Stage Two people keep track of verbal victories and record mistakes, witnesses take sides, and an imaginary debate develops with scores being tallied. The level of commitment required to work through conflict also increases.

Volunteer organizations have difficulty managing conflict at Stage Two because it is easier to walk away rather than maintain the commitment necessary to manage conflict. In private industry alliances and cliques form.

Because the conflict is more complex at Stage Two, problems can no longer be managed with coping strategies. At this stage, the people are the problem. A discussion of issues and answers often proves futile because the people and the problem have become so entangled. You'll also notice resistance when attempts are made to address the issues. To manage conflict effectively at Stage Two, you must implement a people management strategy.

As you work with people, notice the words that are selected to describe conflict or disagreement. At Stage Two conflict, the language is less specific; people talk in generalizations. You'll hear references to the phantom "they" and comments like "everyone believes." Words of exaggeration like "always" and "never" increase in frequency during Stage Two conflict.

Competing parties are less likely to provide accurate facts to one another because the trust level has declined. Questions of "How will you use this information?" become a major concern.

It's important to note that the atmosphere is not necessarily hostile at Stage Two. But it is cautious! Put-downs, sarcasm and innuendoes are survival tactics (but ineffective management tactics) used during Stage Two conflict. Coping strategies like avoidance and obliging that worked so well at Stage One now become ineffective. A "wait-and-see" attitude degenerates into a "you-prove-yourself-to-me" attitude at Stage Two.

You must separate the people from the problem as a first step to managing the conflict at this stage. Here are some ideas:

Ways to Handle Stage Two Conflict

1. Create a safe atmosphere. Provide an environment where everyone is secure:

- Make the setting informal

- Establish neutral turf

- Have an agenda

- Be in control

- Set the tone, be slightly vulnerable

2. Be hard on the facts, soft on the people. Take an extended amount of time to get every detail. Clarify generalizations. Who are "they"? Is "always" an accurate statement? Question whether any fact was missed.

3. Do the initial work as a team, sharing in the responsibility for finding an alternative everyone can live with. Stress the necessity of equal responsibility. Do not carry this load for the group, which is a tendency of conflict managers.

4. Look for middle ground but do not suggest compromise. Compromise implies "giving up" cherished points. Instead, creatively look for the middle ground by focusing on points of agreement.

5. Allow time to pull competing parties toward acceptable ground without forcing issues or concessions.

6. Remember, it is much harder to compete sitting next to someone than across a table. Or sit in a circle.

Stage Two conflict left unchecked will delude thinking and magnify the problems. Conflicting parties see themselves as more benevolent and others as more evil than is actually the case. When you notice comments that focus on either/or, black and white thinking, conflict has escalated into Stage Three.

Characteristics of Stage Three

At Stage Three, the objective shifts from wanting to win toward wanting to hurt. The motivation is to "get rid" of the other party. Conflict has escalated; something must give! Changing the situation and problem-solving are no longer satisfactory for those locked into Stage Three conflict. Being right and punishing wrong become consuming motivations.

Insiders and outsiders are identified by the competing parties as people choose sides on "the issues that matter." Self-interest and the "good of an organization" are equated in the thinking of individuals holding a position in Stage Three conflict.

Leaders emerge from the group and act as spokespersons. Outsiders are enlisted toward the cause, giving little room for middle ground. Small factions evolve, and group cohesiveness is more important than organizational unity.

The merits of an argument and the strength with which positions are held are greatly exaggerated at this stage. A loss of perspective is quite likely on the part of all participants. One tactic you should consider once you observe Stage Three attitudes is the initiation of an intervention team that is neutral to the groups in conflict. For example, members from a disinterested department could be formed to address the concerns and issues of each party. The role of such an intervention team could take the form of mediation or arbitration. During mediation, both sides present their case to the intervention team and the team facilitates discussion and encourages movement toward a mutually acceptable solution. Usually, the opposing parties remain responsible for finding common ground and solutions in mediation.

If consensus cannot be reached, arbitration can be used as a next stage. Each party would present its best case, and one side is selected over the other. There is obviously a great deal to be lost by both sides once this tactic is used, but it can bring an end to high level conflict. Arbitration, especially binding arbitration, demands enforcement. All parties must follow and accept the conclusions of the intervention team or leave!

The members of an intervention team must be perceived as totally impartial, able to provide a fair hearing for everyone. This intervention team will be required to sift through many emotions in search of facts, and they must also provide clear-cut direction at the conclusion of the fact-finding process.

Individuals locked into a Stage Three conflict will likely prolong the conflict, consumed by the event and the energy it provides. Even after management has made its conclusions, some will continue the fight, pursuing their "holy mission."

Negotiation and arbitration are the tools you'll need to bring an end to Stage Three conflict. Negotiation requires parties to sit across from one another and work through the conflict in the presence of an outside agent. This process, once begun, can produce solutions to the problem, but is not likely to produce harmony because at Stage Three, parties have decided that someone must go. At Stage Three, every party loses some ground looking for something workable.

Arbitration takes the negotiation process one step further. Each side presents their best case. The outside agent then selects one or the other. The benefit of this process is that one side is clearly a winner. The disadvantage, of course, is that few companies can afford to have a group of losers!

When conflict escalates to Stage Three, the best strategy you can employ is to minimize the losses and prepare to refocus those who remain.

What do you do with the losers? Possibly replacement or out-placement can be tried. A cooling off period for the losers might also be initiated once a decision is made. It is vital that you have a complete grasp of the negotiation/arbitration process, or you may find you have nothing left to manage.

Ways to Handle Stage Three Conflict

1. Details are important. The outside intervention team must be willing to pay attention to every detail, wading through a considerable amount of negative emotion.

2. Company time must be expended to interview every possible participant.

3. Logic and reason are not effective in dissuading others at this stage. Because everyone will not hold Stage Three intensity in the conflict, identify those individuals who are at the lower stages of conflict and begin redirecting these individuals, providing an alternative source for their energy.

4. Clear corporate goals and a sense of direction will be necessary for individuals to walk away from Stage Three conflict as winners. The good conflict manager delegates tasks to people and redirects events, encouraging the skills of everyone. This is not the time to cover up the event, but it need not be the all-consuming issue individuals have made it out to be!

Summary

The Boy Scout motto, "Be prepared," is excellent advice for conflict management. The following chart can be used as a checklist for assessing conflict.

CONFLICT ASSESSMENT CHECKLIST

STAGE ONE

	YES	NO

1. Are individuals willing to meet and
   discuss facts? ....[ ]..............[ ]
2. Is there a sense of optimism? ....[ ]..............[ ]
3. Is there a cooperative spirit? ....[ ]..............[ ]
4. Does a "live and let live" attitude
   typify the atmosphere? ....[ ]..............[ ]
5. Can individuals discuss issues without
   involving personalities? ....[ ]..............[ ]
6. Are the parties able to stay in the
   present tense? ....[ ]..............[ ]
7. Is the language specific? ....[ ]..............[ ]
8. Do solutions dominate the manage-
   ment efforts? ....[ ]..............[ ]

STAGE TWO

	YES	NO

1. Is there a competitive attitude? ....[ ]..............[ ]
2. Is there an emphasis on winners and
   losers? ....[ ]..............[ ]
3. Is it hard to talk about problems
   without including people? ....[ ]..............[ ]
4. Is the language generalized? ....[ ]..............[ ]
5. Can you identify these statements:
   "They" ....[ ]..............[ ]
   "Everyone is..." ....[ ]..............[ ]
   "You always..." ....[ ]..............[ ]
   "He never..." ....[ ]..............[ ]
6. Is there a cautious nature when issues
   are discussed? ....[ ]..............[ ]
7. Can you detect a "cover-your-hindend"
   attitude? ....[ ]..............[ ]
8. Do the parties make efforts to look good? ....[ ]..............[ ]

STAGE THREE

	YES	NO
1. Are attempts being made to get rid of others?	[ ]	[ ]
2. Is there an intention to hurt?	[ ]	[ ]
3. Have obvious leaders or spokespersons emerged?	[ ]	[ ]
4. Is there a choosing up of sides?	[ ]	[ ]
5. Has corporate good become identified with a set of special interests?	[ ]	[ ]
6. Is there a sense of "holy mission" on the part of certain parties?	[ ]	[ ]
7. Is there a sense that things will never stop?	[ ]	[ ]
8. Has there been a loss of middle ground, allowing only black or white options?	[ ]	[ ]

3
CONSTRUCTIVE
CONFLICT ACTION

Overview

The story of Pinocchio is an excellent reminder about the nature of relationships. Geppetto, the wood carver, wanted a son; so he carved a "wooden boy." But Pinocchio, being wooden, was incapable of making effective decisions; feelings and emotions got in the way. Pinocchio made error after error; his nose growing longer; ineffective in the real world of decisions.

Pinocchio became a real decision maker. The journey was long and painful, but the end result was life. The business manager who begins the journey of conflict management can bring this "life" to any corporation.

Perhaps you've been bogged down by circumstances? Do you often find yourself overwhelmed as you try and keep things together? Like Pinocchio, we need a personal transformation that leads to effective management and powerful decision-making, especially in the face of conflict.

Decision-making is the task of management. A wrong or hasty decision can produce conflict. In addition, the rapid pace of modern business naturally produces conflict. Like Pinocchio, a busy executive must discover a resource for effective decision-making.

If you are going to make the best decisions during conflict, you'll need a healthy understanding of human relationships. Here are seven principles for maintaining positive relationships during conflict.

1. Build Winners; Voting Builds Losers.

The power of positive relationships comes through a management style that builds winners. Voting is a technique used to decide between options, but unfortunately options tend to represent individual desires, especially at higher levels of conflict. A decision to vote can begin a political process where winners and losers begin to keep score.

Should voting be used? Yes, but you should assess the decision being made and consider the ramifications of a choice made by the voting method. How will the losers participate with the new majority? Can a vote be tabled long enough to meet and discuss alternatives with representatives of competing views?

Voting is most effective during lower intensity conflict because the people are problem focused and have less of themselves invested. But voting is too frequently chosen during Stage Two and Three conflict because sides and opinions are easy to count. The "either/or" thinking of Stages Two and Three often promotes the conflict rather than leading to its resolution. One question you should ask is, "Have we exhausted all the options?"

2. Declare a Moratorium.

The declaration of a moratorium is a valuable tool. Relationships are more important than a decision. Roger Fisher, in *Getting Together* says, "If we want a relationship that can deal with serious differences, we have to improve the process itself, independent of the particular substantive problems involved." Time taken to ensure this principle builds a healthy foundation that can tolerate intense conflict.

A moratorium can be declared over issues, problems or decisions. The manager uses time as a resource, deliberately stating intentions and working behind the scenes to ensure the greatest possible outcome. These suggestions could be used to introduce a moratorium...

- "We have some time; let's meet in small groups and look for alternatives."

- "No decision is worth hurt feelings. There are several people who have spent company time and proposed quality ideas. I want to find out why there is such diversity of opinion."

- "The amount of time and energy that have been spent on this issue is significant. We're not ready to decide. A little more time invested now that we've seen the issues might help everyone."

3. Encourage Equal Participation.

Shared responsibility increases ownership. Higher stages of conflict cause individuals to become destructive and lose sight of the organization in favor of personal issues. Opportunities for participation increase the likelihood that individuals will see Level Three conflict as risky — too great a loss.

A simple reminder that "we" are a team can often encourage the desired ownership. You can also share the leadership responsibility by expecting team members to think like a manager in the situation, asking for creative responses to the events that promote cooperation rather than split decisions.

Other examples of shared responsibility include subdividing tasks that generate deliberate barriers of responsibility, and then expecting team leaders to cross the barriers by providing assignments that require cooperative efforts. The importance of shared responsibility is to make the point, emphatically, that no one person owns a problem and everyone shares in the responsibility for solving sticky issues.

Author Thomas Peters' fervor about the need for a service-oriented management style applies during conflict: "We must fundamentally shift our managerial philosophy from adversarial to cooperative." Peters continues, "It is vital to engage in multi-function problem-solving and to target business systems that cross several functional boundaries. Ford and IBM both say they wasted years before realizing that most quality improvement opportunities lie outside the natural work group."

4. Actively Listen

Listening skills cost very little. They are the easiest to learn and can be implemented through sheer desire. People are constantly talking, but too often never stop and listen. All a manager has to do is stop speaking! Listening affirms others in several ways:

1. Listening says you are important, and I'll take time to hear what you have to say.

2. Listening provides quick access to a perspective on conflict.

3. Listening provides data for the manager to make decisions.

4. Listening builds relationships.

Many people are uncomfortable with silence. The effective manager knows that taking time to listen, even if there are periods of silence, is an investment in the relationship. Here are just a few things you can do to fill the silence while tending to the other person:

• Watch the individual's eyes — notice the color.

• Learn to read body language.

• Test yourself after visiting with others. Did you gain as much information as you gave out?

5. Separate Fact From Opinion.

It is easy to believe your position is the truth. At best, an opinion only represents the truth, and far too often opinion reflects perception rather than reality. If you challenge categorical statements and encourage "conditional truth," you will be more effective during higher levels of conflict because the very issues of Stage Two and Stage Three deal with perceptions.

Conditional truth is a philosophical acceptance that the position any person takes is accurate and in the best interest of the company. When we develop a "conditional truth" orientation, it grants every participant the opportunity to be correct and the right to be heard before conclusions are drawn or decisions made.

If you take strong leadership at this point, conflict becomes a matter of separating perspectives rather than challenging liars, a difficult task with adults. But be cautious. Stage Two conflict escalates quickly. Your staff will be ready to blame and accuse rather than work toward resolution, causing a distortion of facts. Conditional thinking will make it harder for individuals to "own" positions.

An additional benefit when you separate fact from opinion is a rise in creativity. Individuals conditioned to consider alternative perspectives are less likely to settle for easy answers. And during confrontation they are more likely to look for options as standard procedure.

Conditional truth is more of an attitude than a process. The effective manager instills a questioning attitude that looks for alternatives rather than debate.

6. Separate People From the Problem.

This is a strategy necessary to manage conflict at any stage. Once the people and the problem are tangled together, a problem becomes unmanageable! Personality problems include a multitude of variables, and many are hard to change.

During conflict it is easy to forget due-process practices. During the higher stages people tend to forget these details. This can result in the early termination of an employee. In business, we must find ways to ensure that details are noticed.

Some may find it difficult to separate the people from the problem, but as a manager you must! Some ideas that can help you separate people from the problem include:

1. Talk in specific rather than general terms.

2. When dealing with Stage Two or Three conflict, use concrete terms and ask for facts.

3. Address conflicting parties as if they have no information. This provides opportunity for them to hear a perspective without having to defend their territory, separating them from the event for a moment.

4. Create a safe environment. The "flight/fight" response is activated during high stages of conflict. Safety enhances the possibilities that individuals will move away from protracted positions.

7. Divide and Conquer.

A great deal of energy is consumed through debate and persuasive tactics. The destructive power that is present during the higher stages of conflict comes when coalitions are formed. Another interesting factor is that as conflict increases, the people involved have a greater need for support. An effective manager has built a team concept and refers to the team at every turn. It is harder for coalitions to form when there is a larger identity. Comments that can point out a team orientation could include, "Superstars make headlines, but are not always easy to work with," or "There is one team in this company."

During conflict it is easy to focus on the negatives. So easy that we tend to act and react in counter-productive ways. Here are five major don'ts:

Five Don'ts During Conflict

1. Don't Get in a Power Struggle. There is a significant relationship between power and authority. Most sociologists acknowledge the fact that as power increases, authority decreases and vice
versa. Well-known sociologist Erik Erikson noted that children
become emotionally disturbed when they possess power they cannot
responsibly handle. Psychologist Emile Durkheim discovered that
clearly defined norms and rules are needed to govern life, or people
become self-destructive.

One creative response you can bring to conflict is an ability to
give away power, allowing others to take control of their feelings and
the event in question.

Your authority increases when you empower others instead of
getting into power struggles. Power tends to be coercive; authority
involves a sense of respect. If you can find a way to turn aside power
struggles, you'll be more effective during conflict. Once a power
struggle begins, three results are possible:

1. The other person is stopped or possibly killed.

2. The other person quits.

3. An ongoing jockeying for position begins.

The end result of power struggles is usually not worth the payoff.
Here are some things you can do to avoid power struggles:

- Don't argue unless you are prepared to waste time. Reason
  won't work.

- Don't engage in a battle unless you are prepared to lose because
  you already have.

- Don't take total responsibility for others' emotions. As the one
  in control, share the responsibility.

2. Don't Become Detached From the Conflict. At first, this may
seem contradictory, but it is actually a way to monitor conflict and
keep it under control. It is important that you have a passionate
concern for both the people and the problem. Business will not
operate without people, and it cannot operate effectively until substantive conflict is managed. Concern is one motivation that drives us
to find the opportunity in conflict.

A macho image of detached leadership provides a distorted perspective too easily imitated and too frequently used. Who wouldn't like to be in charge and have the physical and mental skills to dominate a business situation? Business images of strong-willed Lee Iacocca or free-swinging Donald Trump are just two examples of the "macho businessman" who has complete control and is able to leap tall buildings in a single bound.

The super-power image works in the movies! It works in isolated business dealings and it usually works when we have extreme control of the events and the dollars. Rarely do we have a tailor-made script of power and ability that the movie heroes possess. The tendency to imitate this macho image can deprive you of the natural passion for both your people and your product.

3. *Don't Let Conflict Establish Your Agenda.* Time management specialists suggest it is important for a manager to "do the important and delegate the urgent." This principle is often distorted under the pressure of conflict, and managers are found ignoring many important business matters in an attempt to deal with the conflict.

Perspective is the key. In conflict, as with any management issue, the executive must know both the goals and direction the company is moving. Decisions and responses to conflict should match this overall direction. But sometimes urgent needs interfere with daily schedules. A time study should reveal that you have spent time managing the priorities and not managing conflict unendingly.

Here are some handy tips that can help you manage the urgent:

- Don't spend all your time and energy on one issue.

- Watch time traps. Are there tasks that always seem to consume your time before you're aware it's gone?

- Identify urgent issues, especially negative or conflict issues. If you notice one consistent time offender, manage that offender.

    [ ] Are your people delegating up to you, getting you to do their work?

    [ ] Are they bringing solutions along with concerns?

    [ ] Do they feed your moan-and-groan needs? It's easy to get caught in a negative cycle, and there are always people and events that can feed a "poor me" syndrome.

4. *Don't Be Caught "AWFULIZING."* Joan Borysenko, author of *Minding the Body, Mending the Mind*, defines awfulizing as "the tendency to escalate a situation into its worst possible conclusion." It is easy to be pushed to worse-case scenarios when faced with Stage Two or Three conflict. Those locked into higher levels of conflict lose their ability to quantify the intensity of the problem.

Reminders to Avoid Awfulizing

• People are rarely as benevolent as they perceive themselves to be.

• People are rarely as evil as their opponents perceive them to be.

• Individuals rarely spend as much time thinking about the issues as believed.

• The motivations of others are rarely as planned or thought out as presented. Most aspects of conflict spin off other events and are not the result of coldhearted calculation.

• Every conflict has a history that extends beyond the present. The people and their previous patterns of relating taint the present perception.

5. *Don't Be Fooled by Projection.* Projection is an emotional release. Individuals unconsciously project their own flaws and weaknesses onto others. To be effective during conflict, you should notice the generalizations and accusations being made about others, especially comments about someone's motivations. We may understand others and we may be able to predict their actions accurately, but it is dangerous to believe anyone can read the mind of others.

Summary

Geppetto had a great love for his creation, Pinocchio. According to the fairytale, he traveled far and wide seeking his lost son. When the story ended, there was a miracle — Pinocchio was alive, a real person! The "Seven Principles of Positive Relationships in Conflict Management" and the "Five Don'ts of Conflict Management" mentioned in this chapter are best attempted by those who have a love for their job, their company and its people. The kind of love a woodcarver has for his work.

It's your relationships with people that will determine your success in managing conflict because it will take a "fairytale" type of love to stay on course as you steer through the pain of conflict. But there's also a "fairytale" ending waiting for you!

4

DEVELOPING A
CREDIBLE APPROACH TO
CONFLICT MANAGEMENT

Overview

Conflict has a way of directing itself — too much emotion, too little sense of what to do. A business manager's competency would be seriously questioned if attempts to operate a company were made without a specific plan. But the prevailing attitude during conflict is to fly-by-the-seat-of-the-pants with little thought given to the process, direction or management philosophy.

Conflict can direct a company. This chapter is a road map to conflict management, identifying broad goals that affect the direction of conflict.

Nothing is more frustrating than poor directions! Have you ever been vacationing, stopped for directions and then been sent on a wild goose chase? Conflict places us in a similar setting, one that is strange and uncomfortable. Attempts to manage problems and people often result in a feeling of frustration similar to receiving poor directions.

Conflict Management Requires Clear Decisions

Corporate America has excellent role models like Iaccoca, Uberoth and Geneen. When it comes to business they stand out. They know what to do and when to do it! But they are the exception. Whether it is fear of accountability or a general lack of confidence, many of us lack a sense of direction and purpose, especially during conflict. The tools you need to manage conflict are the same management tools you use daily in business. No matter what management theory you subscribe to – management by objectives, quality circles, Juran's principles of quality or the Japanese management style – all have one common principle. Effective management must be deliberate and move toward a measurable product. Conflict management, although possibly more intimidating, requires this same basic management orientation. The fundamental management principle is to know where you're going!

Conflict does not alter this management philosophy. In fact, conflict calls for the most deliberate and strategic actions you make as a manager.

People look for decisive action during conflict. You appear decisive when you have specific goals and objectives. You must manage the affairs of your company from a position of strength, knowing and then doing what is best to meet your stated purpose.

Whether the issue is boardroom planning or conflict on the production line, to be an effective conflict manager, you must develop a deliberate decision-making process around company goals.

Conflict Management Requires Tolerance for Diversity

Diversity is one resource within every company. The most helpful perspectives are those that differ from our own. Problems arise when alternatives are perceived as a threat. The atmosphere and the degree of tolerance toward diversity will vary with issues and the people involved.

A personal tolerance for diversity encourages you to manage the environment, not the diversity! You become willing to hear people's thoughts and ideas and accept them as a resource. Decisive actions, the type that people want from leaders, tend to be perceived as dictatorial. A tolerance for diversity provides a balance to this perspective. The powerful executive is one who has a solid management philosophy and is not unduly threatened by the presence of competing philosophies.

Conflict tests one's values and attitudes, and reflects an individual's personal commitments:

- Am I sure of myself?

- Have I understood the company and its policies well enough to respond as a manager?

- If I am wrong is there room to learn from my errors?

- Are my actions consistent with my management philosophy?

- Am I willing to allow outsiders to help me in the conflict? (This is an excellent test because if you're worried about looking good, you may be part of a Stage Two conflict!)

Conflict Management Reduces Aggression

An effective executive has an ability to manage the environment, making it safe for self and others. One defense mechanism that is triggered during conflict is aggression, which tends to prompt equally aggressive responses that escalate the conflict. Aggressive managers can be perceived as capricious, making decisions with no real cause or foundation. When you sense aggression, examine the underlying issues:

- Is this a common reaction in these situations?

- Do I have a point to prove/an ax to grind?

- Is this energy properly directed for the event?

- Do other people have the same reaction?

Closely akin to aggression is anger. Anger is a secondary emotion; an initial emotion precedes it. For example, I feel angry that a driver cuts me off in traffic. My initial reaction was that I felt threatened and therefore chose to respond in anger. At the office someone questions the quality of my work and I respond in anger, but my primary emotion was that I felt belittled that my abilities were questioned.

There are times when anger and aggression are important and useful at work. For example, if you must deal with a difficult person and the event requires firm, clear intentions, aggression can be an ally. But this aggressive style should be consciously chosen, not resulting from a reactive emotion.

Words trigger responses in others. You can't control how an individual will "hear" what is said, but you can choose your words carefully to increase understanding. The following words signal aggressiveness and may prompt a counter-productive reaction. Select these words when you need an aggressive response and delete them when you are dealing with a potential conflict event.

- You must (should, ought, better)

- You always or you never

- Don't ask why, just do it

- You know better than that

During conflict, notice if others are being pushy or bossy, demanding center stage, projecting a "know-it-all" attitude. In conflict, the manager can soften aggressive messages by using the following techniques:

1. Remember to share the responsibility. It's hard to be combative with someone who's on your side.

2. Encourage listening; be informed. It's amazing how much you can discover if you will tend to the words of others.

3. Pay attention to excessive self-interest. Winning is for everyone.

4. Make confrontation count. The power of confrontation diminishes with use.

5. A title or position within a company may grant control over people, but true authority involves respect. Respect must be earned. Dictatorial leadership is not conducive to a team philosophy.

6. Anger is short-lived for most aggressive people. There are individuals, however, who don't forget. Enemies created during the resolution of one conflict may be around for the next.

Conflict Management Reduces Passive Behavior

Weak leadership is often passive. The problem with passive management is glossing over things and a loss of respect from co-workers. A passive style is more effective at lower stages of conflict because the coping strategies of avoidance and obliging tend to be passive in nature. If you have a reputation for being indecisive and have a passive management style, the actions you take during higher levels of conflict will probably look feeble to others.

However, the natural characteristics of the passive style can be an asset. The passive style provides an appearance of being distant and unaffected, although the passive manager is usually as frustrated with intense conflict. This outward appearance of calm can be settling to others, but the passive manager must communicate that he is coping with the problem; the issues will be dealt with!

While fear, anxiety and guilt can make any manager ineffective, the passive manager may feel out of control. One technique for enhancing self-confidence is to see how conflict fits the overall direction a department is moving — the "big picture."

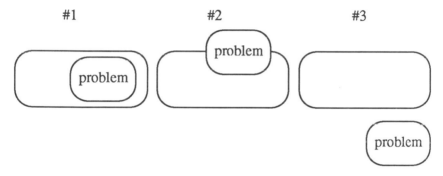

The problem might be part of the big picture, as in #1. Possibly the conflict is only one aspect of the "big picture," as in drawing #2. At other times, the conflict is not related to the "big picture" as in drawing #3. The following statements typify the passive manager and may cause a counter-productive reaction:

- I wish

- If only

- I'm sorry, but

- This is probably wrong

Here are some ideas that can enhance a passive style:

1. Use direct communication (face-to-face) when possible. This demonstrates involvement.

2. Don't respond quickly with agreement. Take some time, even if you don't need it.

3. Interrupt and ask clarifying or probing questions. Be part of the event.

4. Watch for guilt. Guilt is an early warning sign that insecurities exist and that the conflict requires management skills beyond the passive style.

Conflict Management Requires Reduced Manipulative Behavior

Many contemporary management theories encourage a "get-what-you-want" attitude — manipulative philosophy that places self-interest above others. Adopting this philosophy can lead to serious credibility problems.

Here's a quick quiz to test your self-interest quotient:

[ ] Do you find yourself asserting your point of view more often than listening to others?

[ ] Do you worry a great deal about how you look to others? If you do, it can be a sign of self-focus rather than team orientation.

[ ] When team members have a good idea, do you sell them to top management as your own?

[ ] Do you tend to identify team members as expendable commodities that can be pushed and pulled in the manner that best suits a set of goals without regard to their input?

[ ] Do you develop a genuine atmosphere of satisfaction?

The test above is simply a set of indicators. You are the best judge about internal motives and external results. A word of caution must be stated clearly at this point: manipulative management works ineffectively because trust is reduced. A consistent management philosophy, in and out of conflict, is your most effective tool!

5

FIVE STYLES OF
CONFLICT MANAGEMENT

Overview

Adam: "Well Eve, I guess it's too bad we
have to leave this wonderful garden."

Eve: "Yes. I have an uncomfortable feeling
we are entering a period of change."

Change is natural. We have moved through light years in the last century, from kerosene light to electric light and now laser light. We have traveled from horse to space shuttle, and the grocery store has rows of dietary products unknown 10 years ago. Today's $2,000 desktop computer has more power than its $5 million-dollar predecessors that covered an entire floor of an office building. In fact, most of the major inventions have been developed within the last 100 years. If the last 50,000 years were condensed into 50 years it would look like this:

Period of Time	Event
50 years ago	Neanderthal man in prime
10 years ago	People stopped living in caves
5 years ago	Communication via pictures
6 months ago	Printing press invented
1 month ago	Electric lamp invented
3 weeks ago	Wright brothers flew
1.5 weeks ago	First jet flew
1 week ago	First T.V. sold to public
yesterday	First U.S. astronaut in space
seconds ago	Man landed on the moon
nanoseconds ago	U.S. celebrated 200 years' freedom

"Acceleration of Change"
IBM Guide 1976

This rapid rate of change has stretched most relationships, both corporate and individual. The tension generated by change can result in conflict. The process of change and the resulting conflict can be experienced as an inner struggle and identified as intrapersonal conflict. Change also affects organizations. When conflict is experienced between people it is described as interpersonal conflict. You must find techniques for managing both intrapersonal and interpersonal conflict.

The different types of conflict, intrapersonal and interpersonal, will be discussed in this chapter along with five conflict management styles. It is not nearly as important that you know the technical labels and categories of conflict as it is for you to see that conflict can be compartmentalized and dealt with in a systematic approach. First, the types of conflict.

TYPES OF CONFLICT

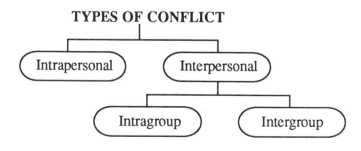

Intrapersonal conflict involves emotional dissonance for an individual when expertise, interests, goals or values are stretched to meet certain tasks or expectations beyond the comfort level. Intrapersonal conflict hampers daily life and can immobilize some people.

When physical, mental or emotional conflict is experienced, it is categorized as intrapersonal conflict. At the mildest levels of intrapersonal conflict, you'll have headaches and possibly backaches. Stress management is a serious antidote for this type of conflict. When we reach the "burnout" levels of stress we are at Stage Two of intrapersonal conflict, and the destructive nature of suicide is an example of a Stage Three intrapersonal conflict.

Interpersonal conflict is more commonly associated with conflict management because it involves groups of people. How an individual copes with conflict (intrapersonal) will determine whether interpersonal conflict can be effectively addressed. Conflict can't be managed externally until you have control of the event internally!

Here are some self-assessment questions to help you determine if intrapersonal conflict is a current issue for you.

1. Are there people you avoid? Avoidance is a coping mechanism and usually signals low levels of stress and conflict.

2. Do you find yourself looking for some release from the day-to-day pressures of work? One school of "pop psychology" has taught that we can vent our feelings and emotions by redirecting the energy into other activities. This works for some. The important point is to be aware of our need to vent our feelings — it's another sign of intrapersonal conflict.

3. Do you find it nearly impossible to get out of a problem-solving mode, even once you've left the office? If we care about an issue, we are more likely to experience stress over its lack of resolution. Conflict is one barometer of our concern. An inability to "put things away" indicates an internal seething common to those struggling with intrapersonal stress.

Don't despair if you answered yes to each of the questions above. Most middle-managers do. Intrapersonal conflict can be a biological alert system that shows you where energy is being drained away and where you need to focus your personal management skills. BUT you must learn to listen to your body:

• Know your blood pressure and cholesterol levels.

• Know which muscle aches are justifiably old age and which ones signal stress and conflict.

• Know who to talk to about your concerns:

1. Do you have people you trust that will listen attentively?

2. Do you have an inner voice that picks you up when you are down? The power of self-talk can make a real difference.

3. Do you know who to go to when you need a "cheering up" and when you need constructive criticism?

4. Do you set aside pride and get professional help when you see that the conflict has escalated to an internal level too great to handle?

Interpersonal conflict is divided into two subgroups: intragroup and intergroup. Conflict that becomes global, emcompassing many groups, is classified as intergroup conflict. However, conflict that stays within the confines of a small group is intragroup conflict. The scope of a conflict determines whether an issue is classified as intragroup or intergroup. Intergroup conflict is the most complex and most serious to an organization. Any time conflict escalates and spreads between groups, the gossip and rumor mill operate and bring harm to you and your business.

It is best to address conflict when it involves only the smallest segment of people. The likelihood of destruction and harm to others increases greatly once multiple personalities become involved.

You can use the chart titled Five Conflict Styles on page 34 as a diagnostic first step. An excellent first step in conflict management is to classify the event and identify what it is doing to you personally, who is involved and whether the conflict has spread from a localized (focused) event to a broader-based conflict involving more people. You can always assume that the increase in people brings generalized problems that are less clearly defined and much more likely to require multiple solutions.

Once you have assessed the involvement of conflict and identified its effects, the next step is to know what strategies can be employed to meet the conflict. There are five universally accepted approaches to conflict management. What's important for every manager is to identify a personal conflict strategy.

Here's a chart I have found helpful:

FIVE CONFLICT STYLES

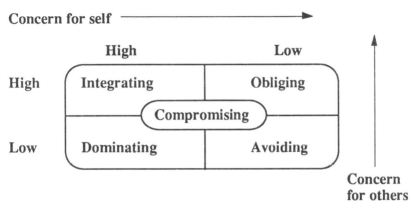

Adapted from A. Rahim's *Organizational Conflict Inventories.*
Consulting Psychologists Press, 1983.

Styles of Conflict Management

The chart above illustrates five conflict styles. An executive with a knowledge of these styles can select a style that is most appropriate for the conflict. It is also possible, once a style is identified, to better understand the motivations of others during conflict.

Integrating is one conflict style. Individuals who choose this style seek an exchange of information. There is a desire to examine differences and reach a solution that is acceptable to all parties. This style is typically associated with problem-solving and is effective when issues are complex.

The integrating style encourages creative thinking. Developing alternatives is one strength of this style. Its emphasis on both self and others synthesizes information from divergent perspectives. However, it is not an effective style when a party lacks commitment or when time is important because integration takes time. It also becomes a frustrating style during higher levels of conflict because reason and rational considerations are often overshadowed by emotional commitments to a position.

Obliging is another style of conflict management. Obliging places a high value on others but a low value on self. This style may reflect an individual's low self-esteem. It's also a strategy you could use to deliberately elevate another person, making them feel better about an issue. This use of obliging by raising another's status is useful, especially if your role within the company is not in a politically precarious position.

The obliging strategy plays down the differences between parties while looking for common ground. The high concern for others causes an individual to satisfy and meet the needs of others, often giving up something of importance to self. Obliging, when used effectively, can preserve a relationship. Obliging used unconsciously can create instant doormats with the words boldly printed, "Please walk over me."

This style is useful if a manager is unsure of a position or fears a mistake has been made. By using the obliging style, the manager passively accepts the power of others, buying time to assess situations and survey alternatives.

Dominating is the opposite of obliging. The emphasis is placed on self. Whereas the obliging individual may neglect his own needs, the dominating style overlooks the needs of others. It is an effective strategy when a quick decision is needed or if a matter lacks importance.

This strategy can be reactionary, activated by self-preservation. It is reflected during an attack championed by the philosophy, "It is better to shoot at 'em than be shot at." When an issue is important, your dominating style will force others to pay attention to a specific set of needs.

The dominating style is helpful if there is a lack of knowledge or expertise. The ability to provide expert counsel or boldly address issues comes from this dominating style. The dominating style is also most frequently associated with the bully and the "hardball tactics" of power brokers.

It is best to use this strategy sparingly. It lasts only as long as you have right and might on your side.

Avoiding is the fourth conflict management style. The avoider does not place a value on either self or others. This is a "don't-rock-the-boat" style.

The negative aspects of the avoiding style include "passing the buck" or sidestepping an issue. A manager using this style will withdraw from the events, leaving others to struggle with the results.

When issues are not important, deferring action allows things to cool off – an effective use of avoidance. It is also an effective style when time is needed. For example, during a board meeting an item can be "tabled" or a postponement called for.

On the other hand, this style can be frustrating for others because answers are slow in developing. Little satisfaction stems from the avoiding style, and conflict tends to run its own course when the avoiding style is used.

Do you have an avoider as your department head? Are you wondering how to get an issue moving? Here are some coping mechanisms and reminders:

1. You cannot care about people who do not care for themselves! You can empathize, love and cajole, but the avoider must have enough concern for self or others before significant movement can take place.

2. Communicate your enthusiasm and hopes. Avoid the negative. Overcome the forces of inactivity by moving in a positive direction.

3. Let them off the hook. Separate the people from the problem for them. Provide a focus on the problem.

4. Play on the avoider's sense of honesty. Seek out and define the reasons for resistance and inactivity.

5. Limit the number of variables presented to the avoider. Place one issue on an agenda, remove others. Make a decision easier by eliminating distractions.

6. Set a deadline.

Compromising is another conflict management style. It is pictured in the center of the Five Conflict Styles chart on page 34, neither high or low in concern for others or self. This is a middle-of-the-road orientation. In compromise, everyone has something to give and something to take. It errs when one side is wrong! It is powerful when both sides are right.

The compromise is most effective as a tool when issues are complex or when there is a balance of power. Compromise can be chosen when other methods have failed and both parties are looking for middle ground. Compromise may mean splitting the difference or exchanging concessions. It almost always means all parties give up something in order to attain resolution.

The five styles of conflict management provide a structure for action. A knowledge of these styles increases your understanding of conflict. There are appropriate times to use each style. Author Gerald C. Meyers provides an excellent analogy of our need and desire to understand conflict styles and prepare for managing conflict:

> Consider, for example, what would happen if you were in a traffic accident on the way to work. The first response of a helpful passer-by is to call for an emergency medical truck. A vehicle soon arrives, staffed by technicians and equipped with a full range of medical supplies and the means to communicate with a nearby hospital.
>
> Paramedics on the ambulance transmit your vital signs to doctors at the hospital so that they can evaluate your condition and devise a plan of treatment while you are in transit. At the emergency room door, you are met by a crew of medical people who already know a lot about you and are ready to administer tests and begin treatment.
>
> At each level the professional's purpose is similar: to gain as much information as quickly as possible and then begin treatment.
>
> Gerald C. Meyers
> *When It Hits the Fan*
> Houghton Mifflin, 1986

You should know the styles of conflict management and choose the best alternative for the situation. This requires an ability to separate your emotions from the event and consciously select a deliberate strategy. Here's a simple list of phrases you can use as verbal cues to trigger the conflict management styles:

Avoidance: • "Can we put this on hold temporarily?"

• "I haven't seen all the facts, I'll get back to you when..."

The avoidance style buys you time. Use it wisely once it's gained. If you notice an individual using this style, it should be a clue that he is uncertain and needs time to investigate the situation. Above all, make it a point to follow up once time is granted. Conflict usually does not go away with time.

Obliging: • "I don't care, whatever you want."

• "You're the expert, what do you think?"

The obliging style gives power to others. If you've got expendable power, it can build trust and confidence in others. If you are secure in your position, it can be used as a method of delegation. The competition is tough in business and few people can afford the luxury of self-deprecating acts. Obliging is not synonymous with humility!

Integrating: • "There seem to be different opinions here, let's get to the bottom of this."

• "Let's get several people from each department together and discuss the options."

The integrating style brings creative juices to the surface and rallies people to find solutions to complex issues. It is excellent when people and the problem are clearly separate, and usually fruitless when people really want to fight. The integrating style can be a positive motivator in brainstorming or problem-solving sessions. But beware – an excluded party from an integrating session can become very disgruntled!

Compromising: • "I can see we have differing opinions. What's your bottom line?"

• "We all have to give and take if we're going to work together, so let's put things on the table."

The compromise style gets the polarities clarified and looks for middle ground. Negotiation and bargaining are complementary skills to the compromise style. The advantage of compromise is that it gets parties talking about the issues and hopefully moves them closer together. Stage One and even Stage Two conflict can employ compromise with some success, but once Stage Three has been reached, retributive actions will need to be defined for the losers.

It will always be difficult to maintain impartiality, and you can expect to be accused of favoritism when this style is used. Rarely can business afford winners and losers, so this is a style that is not recommended unless the losses can be minimized for both sides!

Dominating: • "I don't care, just do what I asked you to do."

• "There are too many issues now, just save money!"

The dominating style gets things done. It is usually power oriented and delivered with force. Power brokers and companies with a strong chain of command tend to favor this style. It usually delineates clearly where the buck stops and who holds responsibility. If you work in a system that frequently manages people and conflict with a dominating style, you'll recognize "cover-your-hindend" thinking as a back-up strategy.

The dominating style is used effectively when there is a great disparity of expertise. The ability to marshal the facts and generate action during conflict can be invaluable. However, the flip side of direct action is incorrect action. Misplaced power can undermine future success.

Summary

There is no right or wrong style. Each style has appropriate uses. Your ability to recognize others' styles and needs can put you well on your way to being a powerful business manager – one who can handle conflict when needed!

6

EMOTIONAL ASPECTS
OF CONFLICT

Overview

Emotions are an integral part of conflict. An understanding of the emotional responses that arise during conflict can make your job easier. Three emotional dynamics of conflict are:

1. The Rejection Response

2. The Interpersonal Gap

3. Emotional Reflexology

The Rejection Response

People follow a predictable sequence in an attempt to deal with the emotional aspects of conflict called the Rejection Response.

THE REJECTION RESPONSE:

1. Anxiety

2. Acceptance

3. A journey inward

   • Flight

   • Fight

4. A balanced reflection

Anxiety

Anxiety is a natural response to change and conflict. Concerns about worth, values and safety are activated. Some people hide this anxious response; others become transparent.

Robert Bridges in his book *Transitions* makes a point that every beginning is preceded by an ending. Even birth, the starting point of life, is preceded by the ending of a symbiotic relationship between fetus and mother. During conflict everyone adjusts to transitions, both the endings and beginnings.

Our anxiety is often encased in fear, and fear is a powerful motivator. It can move an individual away from anxiety toward action. This fear response may or may not be measurable, but it is there! Some people will dig in their heels and protect their present security levels, while others will risk change and explore alternatives. If intervention strategies are to be effective, it must be understood that conflict initially prompts anxiety. Some respond to this anxiety as if it is only a minor irritation (Stage One), but others will protect their comfort zone and fight (Stage Three).

Acceptance

Individuals will reach the acceptance level once the anxiety has passed. A major void exists between anxiety and acceptance, and many conflicts never bridge this gap.

When a person experiences anxiety, one response is to reject the other party. The strength of a relationship is tested at this point, with values clarified and common points of interest examined. One possible conclusion is that the relationship is not worth sustaining. Conflict is resolved by accepting the loss of a relationship.

Volunteer organizations struggle most with this conclusion. For some people, it is easier to join another benevolent group than work through the discomfort of a conflict. Relationships in a volunteer organization are held together by a very thin cord, and change may damage this cord.

A more desired conclusion is an acceptance that things can be dealt with; the people and the product are worth the struggle. Acceptance generates a question of survival reflected in the question, "What's in this for me," followed by an issue of winners and losers. Relationships that produce losers eventually create an unhealthy organization stuck in a cycle of "hurt and be hurt," with a weak commitment among the members.

In conflict, individuals must move away from blame. This movement prompts acceptance. At times acceptance develops slowly, possibly too slowly for some, adding additional stress to the events. But once a level of acceptance is attained, the next step in the Rejection Response follows quite naturally.

A Journey Inward

The journey inward is similar to taking an inventory. Values and concerns are weighed, with each involved party deciding whether it is time to fight, stand up for one's values and concerns, or retreat and wait for a better time. Some psychologists suggest this journey is triggered by self-concept. Others believe it is an instinct that happens in a fleeting moment based on survival. Whatever the motivation, this journey is the growing edge for both the individual and a company. Conflict presents possibility at this phase.

The point of contact between what is and what might be is called the "growing edge." Issues of support and feelings of hopelessness arise now. Some people learn trust if adequate support is discovered, while others step toward despair, unable to find meaning or direction. Some build a world of fantasy while others construct a wall of resistance, never again to be threatened.

During this inward journey the responses arc too numerous for generalizations. What is important for a manager is to apply listening skills during this time. One will identify deep feelings such as rage and anger and share personal values during this time of inner journey. The intensity and diversity of emotions can be a gold mine for a manager aware of conflict management principles. Or these emotions can seem like a snake pit if one is unprepared for conflict management.

Growth and wholeness come through the effective management of inner emotions. As a manager, you can help turn your negative emotions into positive affirmations by using this inner journey.

1. Cherish the freedom to be you. Affirm that you are worthwhile whether raging or calm. Appreciate your anger.

2. Identify negative feelings before they are expressed. Body language is an excellent signal. Listen carefully, discern wisely and focus consciously. Be aware of your anger.

3. Trust yourself. Feel, speak and act spontaneously.   Go with the flow until you find it ineffective or unsatisfying. Trust your anger.

4. Own your thoughts, feelings, words and actions. Others do not make me angry; I choose to be angry. Own your anger.

Balanced Reflection
An awareness of real-world living emerges during the final phase of the Rejection Response. Running from issues means continually running. Fighting never stops, and change seems to continue no matter where one draws the line. This perspective of balance provides the individual with a sense that things can be taken a step at a time.

Stage One conflict is handled regularly by this balanced perspective through the use of coping. Problems arise, but coping determines when and where irritations should be addressed. Permission to cope, manage or ask others to intervene is a balanced response. Stage Two requires management skills. It is more complex, but the balanced perspective sees conflict as an opportunity and not just a destructive force.

Stage Three is managed through intervention, calling on others. The balanced perspective during Stage Three identifies need for outside resources and does not perceive asking for help as a weakness. The balanced perspective identifies areas where growth and possibilities exist. Timing is used effectively as each individual decides whether it is the right time for new journeys.

Summary of the Rejection Response

The Rejection Response is an explanation of the emotional aspects of conflict. The business manager is not a psychologist, but an aspect of effective business management is being aware of these emotional dynamics. Success is not measured by the presence or absence of conflict, but whether you, the manager, are moving the company and your people effectively through issues.

One important element about the Rejection Response is the manager's ability to gain and provide perspective. As one of your team members works through the emotions of conflict, there will be a need to experience each response and learn from it.

The Interpersonal Gap: Communication

Communication is a major problem during conflict. Many issues could be resolved if communication was improved. From an emotional perspective, the loss of communication compounds problems as individuals begin to project what they "believe" are the other side's motivations. This gap between intended message and internally discerned messages contributes to communication problems during conflict.

The Interpersonal Gap

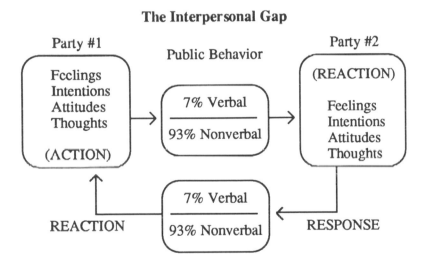

Only 7% of communication is actually transmitted verbally. The bulk of all communication is nonverbal, and creates a natural understanding barrier, usually clarified during dialogue. Facial expressions, body language and the tone of voice play a significant role in our conversations with others. This interpersonal gap arises during conflict as parties struggle to match others' words and actions.

One factor that makes the interpersonal gap more complex is the use of inadequate conflict strategies. The avoidance style employed as a coping mechanism can be interpreted incorrectly. What is intended as toleration of peculiarities might be received as annoyance or lack of concern. A daily irritation becomes a problem — Stage One conflict.

In another instance, rather than debate an insignificant issue, one party might give in by using the obliging style. Party two, assuming a lack of commitment, takes offense. If there has been a history of poor communication, party one might become "one of those people who never cares," and the beginnings of a Stage Two conflict appear.

Words improperly used or vain attempts to spare another's feelings also fall into this interpersonal gap. When an emotion does not match the explanation, the possibility for conflict increases greatly. No one can accurately send or receive communication 100% of the time, which in itself is reason for having a conflict management strategy. Conflict is inevitable given the dynamics of communication. The end result lies in your hands.

Emotional Reflexology

Webster provides two definitions for the word reflex: "Having a backward direction," and "Actions performed by the nervous system involuntarily." When these two definitions are combined, an excellent explanation arises for this emotional dynamic. I call this emotional element of conflict "Emotional Reflexology."

Emotional Reflexology is a movement away from cooperation (turning backward) that involuntarily arises when conflict escalates. Emotional reflexology is characterized by four elements:

1. Blaming

2. Secrecy

3. Repressed feelings

4. Anger

The first is a tendency to place blame. There is an almost instinctive desire to find out "who-dun-it." Our Western emphasis on fairness and equality seems to automatically look for a wronged party. This emotional reaction leads away from a solution and entangles the people and the problem. The drive to place blame decreases responsibility for the problem and elevates one party over others as "blameless." A dichotomized perspective arises around blame rather than solutions.

An example of this blaming response is the all too frequent finger pointing of one department against another. It is easy to identify problems; it is far more difficult to generate opportunities once things have gone wrong. The tendency to place blame generally moves away from a solution because cover-ups and justification absorb much energy.

Another element of Emotional Reflexology is a tendency to be secretive. When facts are most needed, they tend to go underground, held as bargaining chips for later debate. This reaction is accompanied by an inability to remain neutral. Sides gather their facts around polarized positions with an attitude toward protectiveness. This encourages an element of secrecy that thwarts conflict management efforts as conflict escalates.

Most managers quickly identify with this point. People are quick to blame but slow to "rat" on a fellow employee who has a drug or alcohol problem. Rumors that run rampant in the lunchroom are rarely verifiable through the best fact-finding sessions of management. The "secret" factor stifles conflict management efforts.

A third aspect of Emotional Reflexology is a prevailing attitude held by many that feelings are bad and emotions should be held back. Repression of feelings, especially anger, makes provocation possible.

Emotions are a fact, and you have the ability to cope with them. No value should be placed here! When you suppress your emotions, you negate one natural response to the events.

Employees are frequently cheated of both the joy and frustration of top management's reactions to a project's progress. Business may be measured by the bottom line, but people express emotions in response to both success and failure.

The fourth element of Emotional Reflexology deals with perception of anger. Anger, when vented at lower stages of conflict, can bring about a catharsis, helping the parties identify issues and values involved. But anger expressed during higher stages of conflict has the opposite effect. Emotional Reflexology causes us to employ anger inappropriately, using anger at higher stages and avoiding it at lower stages, exactly the opposite of its proper use.

The inappropriate use of anger may stem from rising frustration over a conflict and cause an explosion of emotions resulting in unwanted words and misplaced blame. Others have an inordinate desire to "look in control" and suppress their anger early in a conflict. In both cases, at lower stages of conflict Emotional Reflexology causes us to squelch anger, assuming it will pass.

During higher stages of conflict, we finally exceed our toleration level and express the anger, usually inappropriately. Once higher stages of conflict are reached, it is obvious that everyone is angry and the anger serves little value. One excellent management technique for handling anger in the higher stages of conflict is to say: "It is clear that everyone is angry, but it will help us little to escalate our emotions. I recognize your anger and will seriously consider your concerns. There is no longer a need to vent those emotions in this setting."

The proper focus of anger is at issues, not at people — something hard to remember once the people and problem are intertwined. Along with anger is the threat of danger to other parties. If anger is expressed at Stage Three, it can be dangerous since the goal is to get rid of the other party.

Here's a checklist you can use as a tool to sharpen your awareness of the emotional issues identified in this chapter.

EMOTIONAL ISSUES CHECKLIST

Create a Safe Environment

Yes	No

1. Have you shared hope and optimism?

2. Did you communicate that this is manageable?

3. Is it clear that no one needs to be hurt?

4. Did you communicate a concern for everyone's success?

5. Have you established equality:

   • Put-downs not allowed?

   • No punishments will be made?

   • All feelings are acceptable?

6. Did you communicate that all involved will survive?

Meet the Intrapersonal Needs of Others

Yes | No

1. Did you communicate, "I care about you"?

2. Did you communicate, "I care about our relationship"?

3. Did you communicate, "I care about this company"?

4. Did you communicate, "I want you to have some input in how this will be resolved"?

Join the Issue...Invite...Confront

Yes | No

1. "We (not you) have a problem."

2. "Let's get started together."

3. Have you listened?

   • Do you know as much about the other party as your own position?

   • What are the facts?

   • What are the feelings?

4. Have you separated fact from opinion?

5. Are you assuming or do you know?

6. What are the vested interests?

7. Are there multiple solutions?

7

EFFECTIVE INTERVENTION IN CONFLICT MANAGEMENT

Overview

The airline pilot has power at his fingertips: millions of dollars in equipment and hundreds of lives at stake with every movement.

Behind the scenes is a flight crew, less visible to the general public, but just as responsible. There is also a ground control crew and a control tower crew.

There is a cadre of company officials, travel agents and airport staff who provide a multitude of services.

It's easy to praise the pilot for a pleasurable flight, but without thousands of other people, a positive end result would be impossible.

The analogy above applies equally to conflict management. An effective intervention strategy begins with a humble awareness that "super-human" skills are inadequate without the cooperation of others — so teamwork is essential to effective conflict management.

Negotiation and mediation are used during the higher stages of conflict. Usually a negotiation or mediation team comes from outside conflicting groups.

This intervention team does not necessarily need to be outside the company, but must be perceived by both parties as authoritative and capable of dealing fairly with all the issues. All parties should have a part in the selection process of an intervention team.

Selecting an Intervention Team

1. Make a list of potential members. This list should include at least three times as many names as will be appointed to the team.

2. Provide both sides with a resume on each individual.

3. On a specified date representatives from each conflicting party will meet. Alternating between parties, each group will be allowed to delete one name from the list. This process will continue until only the predetermined number is left.

4. The names that endure this process will be the intervention team.

The presence of an intervention team is evidence that things have escalated beyond the workable stage. Events must be controlled by an external source. The following guidelines can be helpful in establishing the intervention team.

Guidelines for an Intervention Team

Limit Hostility.   There is little need for hostility once the intervention team is selected. Their presence is an indication that lines are severely drawn. A deliberate de-escalation of hostility by the intervention team can be helpful in moving the conflict to more manageable stages of conflict.

Become Involved.   The intervention team is capable of providing insight and creative alternatives. Lower-level conflict requires participation in the final outcome. Once Stage Three conflict has been reached, resolution is mandatory. Ownership in a negotiated or mediated settlement comes with the exit of the intervention team.

Get a Note-Taker.   The intervention team should secure an accurate note-taker rather than function in this capacity. The attention necessary to record the details can distract from efforts to resolve the conflict.

Brevity in Explanations.   The intervention team will provide feedback during the process. This is a time for clear, clean, crisp and factual reporting, not for speeches or lengthy explanations.

Shun Confidentiality.   The intervention team will not deliberately violate individual positions, but the process of data gathering is extensive. The need to maintain confidentiality can inhibit the effectiveness of the intervention team. There is also a tendency on the part of the conflicting parties to "tone down" threats and accusations when confidentiality is not guaranteed, de-escalating the mood of a Stage Three conflict.

Avoid Being a Rescuer.   The intervention team offers only an external third-party perspective. It is easy to promise more than can be delivered during conflict management. People are willing to give the intervention team responsibility for solving problems and rescuing the company. Expectations run high once an intervention team has been identified. This expectation places undue pressure on the intervention team, often without an accompanying amount of pressure placed on the disputing parties. The responsibility for resolving the conflict remains with the disputing parties.

Begin an Accountability Process.   Once an agreement has been reached through intervention, follow-up will be necessary to encourage and monitor compliance. An early focus on accountability can make the follow-up process easier.

Statements about issues or people must be accurate. Conflict exaggerates issues and facts. The intervention team must be willing to confront categorical positions and ask if an individual is willing to be quoted on a point.

Deal With Rumors or Accusations Directly.   During high intensity conflict, a separation of people and problem is essential. One technique an intervention team can employ is to generate face-to-face dialogue. Rumors abound during higher stages of conflict. The following steps help control unsubstantiated statements.

Step One: Ask if an individual is willing to go with you and discuss the issues face to face.

Step Two: If he refuses, ask if you can use his name and approach the other party with the facts expressed.

Step
Three: If he refuses, state categorically that there is no point in addressing this issue further, and you will not acknowledge any perspective based on these facts.

The Intervention Process

A Five-Stage Mediation Process

1. Establish the parameters

2. Collect the data

3. Frame the issues

4. Generate alternatives

5. Evaluate and agree

This five-step process is a suggested format for conducting a third-party intervention. The success or failure of this format resides with the parties involved. However, an effective intervention team can serve as a catalyst to action and resolution even at the highest conflict stages.

Establish the Parameters

It would be great if people and companies conducted themselves according to proper etiquette. Unfortunately, they don't! The intervention team must define standard operating procedures. Establishing ground rules builds credibility for the intervention team and can be used to set a positive tone.

Basic Ground Rules for the Intervention Team

1. Everyone will be asked to speak in personal terms, using "I" statements rather than blaming or attacking others. The goal of the intervention team is not to affix blame but to find a solution.

2. Assumptions of behavior will be accepted with skepticism. The intervention team is looking for verifiable facts. Once statements are made, they will seek out the truth and confirm or deny it.

3. The intervention team will not become a filter for information that cannot be shared or verified. Confidentiality leads to inside information that is counter-productive to resolution.

4. Threats are not acceptable. The presence of an intervention team indicates that serious problems exist. Excessive hostility undermines resolution.

5. The intervention team is here to act as a catalyst for resolution. They are not the ones who will solve problems. Problems must be solved by those involved; however, the intervention team does have an outside perspective that can be helpful.

6. The intervention team will conduct interviews, distribute questionnaires and hold public information meetings as needed. Everyone will be kept informed. Conflicting parties will be asked to cease all comments until the intervention team has completed its findings.

Collect the Data

The intervention team needs to gather information in a short amount of time. The conflicting parties should be able to provide a list of initial contacts that would be able to provide information. Information that should be collected includes:

- A history of the conflict

- Communication patterns

- A distribution of perceived power

- The priority of the problem in relation to company or unit goals

The intervention team has two avenues for collecting information: a questionnaire and personal interviews.

Interviews

Listening techniques are of utmost importance during interviews. The interviewer should provide nonverbal support because efforts to reassure the parties can reduce anxiety and move toward an acceptance of the events. Fairness, empathy, openness and a sincere sense of objectivity should characterize the interview.

"Conflict listening" is a specific listening skill that provides adequate support to the speaker while clarifying feelings and content. The chart below illustrates conflict listening, a two-step process of defuse and reframe.

Conflict Listening

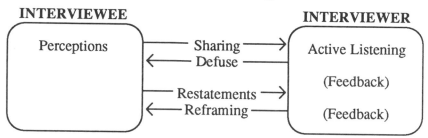

The first step, defuse, is designed to hear everything an individual brings to the conflict. Many emotions, some extremely heightened, must be sifted through. Once these emotions have been identified, the interviewer speaks back to the party toning down (defusing) the emotions, separating the people from the problem.

There is no guarantee that the interviewer can move to reframing. Some will not desire or be able to separate people from problem. Others will de-escalate once they have been heard. The interviewer then identifies an impasse or defuses the situation.

Reframing involves a synthesis of issues and positions that accurately reflects an individual's perceptions, balanced by the interviewer's perspectives. Concessions can be identified for later use.

The interviewer is looking for the core issues, which will not be the same for everyone. Core issues, once collected, can be presented in a public meeting (framing), as part of the "significant findings."

Reframing the Issues

The difference between reframing and framing is the arena. Reframing happens during individual or small group interviews. Framing takes place in a public meeting. During framing the intervention team enters the process, providing guidance and direction.

Author Edward de Bono categorically states, "The parties involved in a dispute happen to be in the worst possible position to settle that dispute." He continues, "If you are too closely involved in a situation, it is difficult to get an overview or to get a sense of perspective." The intervention team therefore brings the best available insight to a conflict. This process of intervention is not simply passive administration or a rehashing of problems. The role of the intervention team is to design a solution that meets the needs of the group and encourage movement toward a positive use of the conflict.

The interview team frames the issues within a context of options. Conciliatory remarks can be suggested along with a wide range of alternatives. Framing is limited only by the creativity of the intervention team. The intention is to move the opposing parties toward convergent points of view.

Generate Alternatives

A pilot was asked why cabin lights are dimmed prior to night landings. His response, "We prepare for a worst-case scenario. Since the landing presents the possibility of a crash, we want our passengers to be accustomed to the dark if the worst happens. Their eyes will be adjusted to the darkness so they can see to exit the plane."

Many people are shocked by worst-case scenarios. Yet the destructive nature of a Stage Three conflict can result in a worst case. The direct presentation of worst cases is a valuable and dramatic illustration of the need for resolution.

Another option is the "cheap shot," named for its quick and almost off-the-cuff response. Once in a while, a quick idea flashes across a room that has within it resolution. Without resorting to a vote, the intervention team can poll the group and test an option. If it flies, the beginnings of a working solution can be formulated.

Few Stage Three conflicts are single issues. There are usually many points with varying degrees of agreement and disagreement. The intervention team can move away from polarization while generating options by listing the points of convergence.

The atmosphere shifts from intervention-controlled to group-owned at this point. After several ideas have been presented by the intervention team, the floor is gradually opened to input.

Negative and reactionary feelings may arise, and the intervention team must be willing to stop all input with a quick comment such as, "That has been heard, and we have attempted to deal with it in our presentations. Please help us focus on the future now."

Once ideas have run out and the best alternatives appeared, the intervention team should call a break, move to a different room and begin the process of sifting through the issues.

The new setting should have a conciliatory atmosphere with a "big picture" perspective. Make banners, signs and fliers that describe the reason the group exists. Seating should be circular rather than face to face. It is harder to polarize around a round table!

The intervention team must take charge, providing very specific leadership. Work with the easy issues first. There is a cumulative effect that builds as parties spend time working on a solution. The longer people remain in the process, the more they tend to be invested in an answer. Once the easy concessions have been defined, the core issues can be addressed.

The core issues — those concerns that present major discord — may still present problems. The intervention team must present an "openness" to all points. As convergence happens, some will feel they are looking into a tunnel that is getting narrower. This "squeeze" must reflect new directions rather than a loser's perspective. A new group has formed and "we" are headed into new territory together. If the process breaks down, worst-case scenarios can be represented.

Last-resort options include voting on the alternatives. One side wins and the other loses. Losers are informed before this strategy that they MUST comply if they lose. Generally compromise is more appealing once the alternatives of "all-win" or "all-lose" are presented.

Compromise is left as a last resort option because it reflects no winners. In a compromise solution there are "almost winners" and "almost losers." The compromise is perceived as a tie. Once a conflict has reached Stage Three, ties usually are not satisfying for anyone, but they may be better than losing everything!

Stage Three conflict is polarized around personalities. Leaders and spokespeople are apparent, but the intervention team does not want to encourage conferences by these spokespersons. Keep the solution contained within the group of representatives until it is agreed upon. It will be the role of the intervention team and the spokespeople to present the results to the parties.

Evaluation and Agreement

Although the decision has been hammered out by the parties and the intervention team, a sales job must follow. The rest of the company must be informed of the decision.

First, spokespersons from all perspectives must be seen together at the front of the room with a member of the intervention team. True ownership is communicated when all those involved in the decision stand together and explain the conclusions.

DO NOT allow the spokespeople to speak privately to their own group. It is easy, in a face-saving manner, to project a "this-is-the-best-we-could-do" attitude. The intervention team and spokespeople want to communicate that "this is a great alternative to our problem."

The second point of evaluation and agreement is to delineate when and where people may go to pursue the conclusion in private. The intervention team must be willing to enter into a defuse and reframe position with those most intensely involved. This requires a very firm hand on the part of the intervention team. This defuse and reframe time should be conducted in the presence of a member from all sides and led by a member of the intervention team.

A letter of consensus should be drafted by the head of the intervention team. This letter lists in a positive manner the conclusions that have been reached. This letter includes these three areas:

1. We met...

2. We discussed...

3. We did...

Finally, the management staff that initiated the formation of an intervention team should have developed an "along-side" strategy for business over the past weeks that provides time to work with people across the barriers that have developed. Management must be creative in developing workable, positive interactions. The key to moving in a positive direction is an emphasis on the "new team"!

Here are some suggestions in building an "along-side" plan:

1. Identify individuals from both sides that are not affected by the conflict.

2. Identify people who have the greatest investment in losing, and seek a "buy-in" from them to work toward meaningful results.

3. Find ways to generate meaningful teamwork and work toward the completion of short-term company, department or division goals.

4. Disputants that are entrenched in Stage Three should be identified and given short-term, easy-to-complete tasks. This builds confidence and provides opportunity to suggest that until the conflict is settled favorably for everyone, the risk of extensive involvement in team projects and goals would be unwise.

5. Establish a "big picture" focus that clearly identifies to all parties that the company is larger than the conflict. Foster an attitude that things will continue and that people are expected to work with one another.

CONCLUSION

The spectrum of conflict is broad, and the methods for addressing conflict diverse. The good news about conflict management is that the strategy you use in the day-to-day management of your people and company is the same strategy you should use to manage conflict.

I wanted this handbook to encourage you to bring your management skills into the arena of conflict, and I hope you found something practical that will help you on the job.

Two charts are included as a summary. Each provides an overview of conflict. The first chart lists the classic dispute resolution models. It has helped me to see the range of emotions and actions available during conflict. Too often, I narrow my focus and miss the alternatives because I take the short view.

The second is a summary. The "Seven C's" chart encapsulates the concepts we have discussed throughout this handbook. They can be kept as quick reference points or used as a checklist.

Classic Dispute Resolution Models

Fight

Violence

Non-Violent Overthrow

Legislation

Court
    (imposed 3rd party)

Arbitration

Mediation
    (voluntary 3rd party)

Negotiation
    (management skills)

Discussion
    (problem-solving skills)

Toleration
    (coping skills)

Flight

The Seven C's of Conflict Management

CHARACTERISTICS

Specific characteristics are common to all conflict. Once you're aware of these characteristics, you can chart the unknown and explore the territory.

CLASSIFICATION

Conflict can be classified. If you identify the conflict, it's possible to respond with the most appropriate management strategy.

CONSTRUCTIVE

Positive actions are the best response to negative events. You can be constructive during destructive events. Winners win and good managers are productive, even during conflict!

CREDIBILITY

Your credibility as a manager increases when issues are addressed in a thoughtful and consistent manner. One goal during conflict management is to create credibility by matching modern business strategies with conflict management strategies.

CONDITIONAL

No two conflicts are the same. People change and so do issues. The conditional nature of conflict makes it imperative that you develop a variety of styles and be able to meet the changing dynamics of business.

CARE

Fear is a natural response to change and conflict, but it need not inhibit business. You care about your business and the people you work with. The emotional elements of conflict management prompt emotional reactions that are unpleasant, but they too can be managed.

CONSTRAINT

External resources are needed at times to keep things in perspective. The constraint factor encourages you to use an intervention team when conflict escalates to threatening levels.

Suggested Reading

The following books were referenced in this text and contain excellent resource materials for further study.

Bramson, Robert. *Coping With Difficult People.* New York, NY: Ballantine Books, 1981.

Campolo, Anthony. *The Power Delusion.* Wheaton, IL: Victor Books, 1983.

deBono, Edward. *Conflicts: A Better Way to Resolve Them.* New York, NY: Penguin Books, 1985.

de Bono, Edward. *de Bono's Thinking Course.* New York, NY: Facts on File Pub., 1982.

Dyer, William G. *Team Building: Issues and Alternatives.* Reading, MA: Addison-Wesley, 1977.

Fisher, Roger and William Ury. *Getting to Yes: Negotiating Without Giving In.* New York, NY: Houghton-Mifflin, 1982.

Fisher, Roger and Scott Brown. *Getting Together: Building a Relationship That Gets to Yes.* New York, NY: Houghton-Mifflin, 1988.

Hart, Lois. *Learning From Conflict.* Reading, MA: Addison-Wesley, 1981.

Leas, Speed. *Discover Your Conflict Management Style.* Washington, D. C.: Alban Institute, 1985.

Myers, Gerald. *When It Hits the Fan.* New York, NY: Houghton-Mifflin, 1986.

Peters, Thomas. *Thriving on Chaos.* New York, NY: Knopf Pub., 1987.

Rahim M. Afzalur. *Rahim Organizational Conflict Inventories.* Palo Alto, CA: Consulting Psychologists Press, 1983.

INDEX

Notes

Notes

Notes

Notes

Notes

Notes

Each of our handbook series (LIFESTYLE, COMMUNICATION, PRODUCTIVITY and LEADERSHIP) was designed to give you the most comprehensive collection of hands-on desktop references all related to a specific topic. They're a great value at the regular price of $12.95 ($14.95 in Canada); plus, at the unbeatable offer of buy two at the regular price and get one free, you can't find a better value in learning resources. **To order**, see the back of this page for the entire handbook selection.

1. Fill out and send the entire page by mail to:

National Press Publications
6901 West 63rd Street
P.O. Box 2949
Shawnee Mission, Kansas 66201-1349

2. Or **FAX 1-913-432-0824**

3. Or call toll-free **1-800-258-7248**

Fill out completely:

Name _____

Organization _____

Address _____

City _____

State/Province _____ ZIP/Postal Code _____

Telephone (   ) _____

Method of Payment:

☐ Enclosed is my check or money order
☐ Please charge to:
　☐ MasterCard　☐ Visa　☐ American Express

Signature _____ Exp. Date _____

Credit Card Number

☐☐☐☐☐☐☐☐☐☐☐☐☐☐☐☐

To order multiple copies for co-workers and friends:	U.S.	Can.
20-50 copies	$8.50	$10.95
More than 50 copies	$7.50	$ 9.95

VIP# 705-008495-092

OTHER DESKTOP HANDBOOKS

	Qty.	Item #	Title	U.S.	Can.	Total
LEADERSHIP		410	The Supervisor's Handbook, Revised and Expanded	$12.95	$14.95	
		458	Positive Performance Management: *A Guide to Win-Win Reviews*	$12.95	$14.95	
		459	Techniques of Successful Delegation	$12.95	$14.95	
		463	Powerful Leadership Skills for Women	$12.95	$14.95	
		494	Team-Building	$12.95	$14.95	
		495	How to Manage Conflict	$12.95	$14.95	
		469	Peak Performance	$12.95	$14.95	
		418	Total Quality Management	$12.95	$14.95	
COMMUNICATION		413	Dynamic Communication Skills for Women	$12.95	$14.95	
		414	The Write Stuff: *A Style Manual for Effective Business Writing*	$12.95	$14.95	
		417	Listen Up: *Hear What's Really Being Said*	$12.95	$14.95	
		442	Assertiveness: *Get What You Want Without Being Pushy*	$12.95	$14.95	
		460	Techniques to Improve Your Writing Skills	$12.95	$14.95	
		461	Powerful Presentation Skills	$12.95	$14.95	
		482	Techniques of Effective Telephone Communication	$12.95	$14.95	
		485	Personal Negotiating Skills	$12.95	$14.95	
		488	Customer Service: *The Key to Winning Lifetime Customers*	$12.95	$14.95	
		498	How to Manage Your Boss	$12.95	$14.95	
PRODUCTIVITY		411	Getting Things Done: *An Achiever's Guide to Time Management*	$12.95	$14.95	
		443	A New Attitude	$12.95	$14.95	
		468	Understanding the Bottom Line: *Finance for the Non-Financial Manager*	$12.95	$14.95	
		489	Doing Business Over the Phone: *Telemarketing for the '90s*	$12.95	$14.95	
		496	Motivation & Goal-Setting: *The Keys to Achieving Success*	$12.95	$14.95	
LIFESTYLE		415	Balancing Career & Family: *Overcoming the Superwoman Syndrome*	$12.95	$14.95	
		416	Real Men Don't Vacuum	$12.95	$14.95	
		464	Self-Esteem: *The Power to Be Your Best*	$12.95	$14.95	
		484	The Stress Management Handbook	$12.95	$14.95	
		486	Parenting: *Ward & June Don't Live Here Anymore*	$12.95	$14.95	
		487	How to Get the Job You Want	$12.95	$14.95	

SALES TAX
All purchases subject to state and local sales tax. Questions? Call **1-800-258-7248.**

Subtotal	
Sales Tax (Add appropriate state and local tax)	
Shipping & Handling ($1 one item, 50¢ each add.)	
Total	